Write to Restore

Write to Restore

A Step-By-Step
Creative Writing Journal
for Survivors of Sexual Trauma

Jen Cross

Mango Publishing
CORAL GABLES

Cover Design: Roberto Nuñez
Cover Photo/illustration: Charcompix (Shutterstock)
Layout & Design: Roberto Núñez

For permission requests, please contact the publisher at:
Mango Publishing Group
2850 S Douglas Road, 2nd Floor
Coral Gables, FL 33134 USA
info@mango.bz

For special orders, quantity sales, course adoptions and corporate sales, please email the publisher at sales@mango.bz. For trade and wholesale sales, please contact Ingram Publisher Services at customer.service@ingramcontent.com or +1.800.509.4887.

Write to Restore: A Step-By-Step Creative Writing Journal for Survivors of Sexual Trauma

Library of Congress Cataloging-in-Publication number: 2019948612
ISBN: (print) 978-1-64250-106-3, (ebook) 978-1-64250-107-0
BISAC category code SELF-HELP / Abuse

Welcome, welcome.

I am so glad that you are here:
alive and healing,
at the page, and ready to write.

Table of Contents

Introduction *8*

WEEK ONE
Beginnings *16*

WEEK TWO
Conversations with the Body *26*

WEEK THREE
Myths and Truths *36*

WEEK FOUR
Reclaiming Voice *46*

WEEK FIVE
Writing into Spirit *56*

WEEK SIX
Welcoming Our Desire *66*

WEEK SEVEN
Reaching Back Through the Fire *76*

WEEK EIGHT
Radical Self-Care *86*

Additional Prompts *96*
Further Reading About Writing and Transformation *120*
About Jen *124*

Introduction

Our words restore us, and our writing can "re-story" our lives.

In a quiet morning bedroom, on the bus or subway on the way to work or school, in the laundromat while waiting for the spin cycle to complete, at a kitchen table, at innumerable cafes—over and over, throughout the country, around the world—people are sitting down to write.

Early morning, over lunch breaks, during the wee hours of the night: we who have experienced something that interrupted our sense of self, we who have been irrevocably harmed or violated, we who experienced something so outside our normal, our understanding of ourselves, that we lost even the language to try and express it—we are turning to the page. We who had language taken from us, we whose words were ignored or denied, we who were hurt even before we had the words for what was being done to us—we reach for words anyway.

We are a species made of words and stories. When we are without language for ourselves and our lives, we often feel profoundly disconnected from our communities, even from the rest of humanity.

Writing can be:

- a way to release images and experiences that have been held in our bodies for years

- a way to discover what we didn't know we knew

- a way to re-story ourselves and our lives

- a way to regain trust in our creative instinct and voice

- a way to heal in body and mind

As you reach for words, sometimes it is helpful to have someone with you. This journal guides you through a series of exercises I first developed for the Write Whole survivors' writing group, offered through my organization, Writing Ourselves Whole.

In this guided workbook, a companion to my book *Writing Ourselves Whole: Using the Power of Your Own Creativity to Recover and Heal from Sexual Trauma*, we'll move loosely through a series of themes, beginning gently before shifting to more intense writing midway, then broadening out to connect with community and self-care.

Week One: Beginnings—In week one, we warm up our writing hands with a couple of short writing exercises that invite us to practice freewriting.

Week Two: Conversations with the Body—In week two, we drop into these bodies that sustain us: what untold, unsung stories do we carry under our skin?

Week Three: Myths and Truths—Many of the stories told about sexual trauma survivors are based on lies and denial, and they can harm our understanding of ourselves, our survival, and our healing. In week three, we examine, unpack, and *re-story* those myths.

Week Four: Reclaiming Voice—Our voices are a core part of who we are. In week four, we think about the ways our voices have been ignored or denied, and we talk back, speak up, and demand to be heard.

Week Five: Writing into Spirit—Spirit is a complicated concept for many of us, but we may want to connect with something outside of ourselves bigger than we are, whether a god or nature or community. In week five, we make some space on the page to speak to spirit and listen to what she has to say back.

Week Six: Welcoming Our Desire—We who are survivors of sexual trauma may have extremely mixed feelings about our desires, especially our sexual desires. In week six, we gently write into some of those hungers, considering what our bodies want and how we can most tenderly claim that touch, if and when we choose it.

Week Seven: Reaching Back Through the Fire—In week seven, we consider those people and voices that show us what survival could look like. What can we "pay forward" to the survivors coming up after us?

Week Eight: Radical Self-Care—What does it mean to care for something that has been misused or harmed? Taking care of ourselves is a profoundly political and radical act, as Audre

Lorde told us a long time ago. In our closing week, we write into the possibility and joy of loving what we were taught to despise.

The Task Ahead

Journal writing can be a practice that changes us, helping us to find language for fragmented experiences within us that feel incomplete. This book is a tool as you grow your own practice—use it in any way that best serves you, your words, your writing, your healing.

Make the prompts work for you. Sometimes, if you're stuck, you might want to try changing the pronoun in the prompt. Most of these prompts are in the first-person singular ("I"), but you can change to first-person plural ("we"), the second person ("you"), or the third person ("she/he/they"). See how the writing changes when the point of view changes. If you get stuck while you're writing, you can start over with the same prompt, make the prompt a negative (instead of "How would you tell this story?" think "How would you not tell this story?"), or use the phrase, "What I really wanted to write about was…"

You might use this book alone, going straight through the eight weeks, responding to two prompts per week, just as we'd do in a writing workshop. You might open the journal at random, allowing a prompt to select you. If you find yourself opening to a prompt you've done before, that's ok. In my experience, something new emerges when an old prompt is revisited.

You can write in partnership with a collaborator, a friend, or another survivor. You might also choose to write in a circle with a group of others. You can write together and then read aloud what you've written (if you choose to). You can talk about the process if you like or discuss things that came up for you during the writing.

If you are bringing a group together, you might wish to read through the Witness section of *Writing Ourselves Whole* (and, in particular, the chapter "DIY Wit(h)ness: Ideas for Gathering Your Own Group") for things to consider when co-creating a space that serves and holds all writers and writing, a space for risk and discovery and generosity.

As you move through this journal, I'll encourage you to be gentle with yourself. There's no right or wrong way to freewrite, just as there's no right or wrong way to heal from trauma.

Listen to your body, listen to your intuition, and trust your creative wisdom. Try not to push yourself. If it takes longer than eight weeks to move through these exercises, that's just fine! If you start writing along with a prompt and then your writing goes in a completely different direction, please listen to your writing rather than the prompt.

Try and allow yourself to feel whatever emotions rise up in you as you write; there's no wrong way to feel while you do this. And be kind to yourself after writing: rest, give yourself a little sun, cuddle a beloved animal friend, watch silly TV—this isn't work that gets accomplished in an afternoon. Transformation, like healing, takes time, and it's the work of our life. Give yourself space, and trust your own process.

If you want to use this journal to build a regular writing practice:

See if you can write at the same time every day (or most days). Once you settle into a routine and make writing a habit in your life, you'll probably find your creative flow begins to rise to meet you about that time every day. And on days the flow is more of a trickle, write anyway: it keeps the writing muscles loose, and it communicates to your writing self that you're a trustworthy partner in this process. Try not to wait for inspiration before you sit down and write. Lots of writers describe the way inspiration tends to find them more frequently when they are dedicated to their daily practice.

What works best for some folks is to write just after waking up, before they engage in any other reading or media intake, while they're still close to that dream state. Others find that their creativity kicks in in the evening after all the activity of your household has quieted down. Another group prefers to write in the middle of things: on the subway, at the laundromat, or in a bustling cafe. Sometimes folks prefer to have music playing or the noise of other peoples' conversations around them; others need it quiet. If you're not sure what works best for you, try writing at different times and in different locations. Trust what feels right, even if it's different from what other writers in your community prefer.

Try on freewriting as a practice: once you start writing, keep writing for the time you've set for yourself, no matter what. If you get stuck, write "I'm stuck" or "I don't know what to write" or just repeat the last thing you wrote until other words offer themselves up. Follow your writing wherever it leads you: trust your words, don't stop to censor yourself or edit what you've written, and try not to direct the flow.

Week One

Beginnings

We begin gently, easing ourselves onto the page, reminding our hands what it's like to be with the pen or keyboard, reminding our bodies what it's like to be with words.

Set your timer for seven minutes, and begin with the phrase, "My favorite time and place to write is…"

Other introductory prompts you might try:

- This is when I knew I liked to write…

- These were words I loved as a child/these were words I hated as a child…

- This was the first book I loved…

- These were the stories I heard as a child…

- I write in order to…

You may be familiar with the George Ella Lyon poem, "Where I'm From," which begins like this:

> *I am from clothespins,*
> *from Clorox and carbon-tetrachloride.*
> *I am from the dirt under the back porch.*
> *[…]*
> *I am from the forsythia bush*
> *the Dutch elm*
> *whose long-gone limbs I remember*
> *as if they were my own.*

Another "Where I'm from" poem, this one by Willie Perdomo, includes these lines:

> *If I said that I was from 110th Street and Lexington*
> *Avenue, right in the heart of a transported Puerto Rican*
> *town, where the hodedores live and night turns to day*
> *without sleep, do you think then she might know where*
> *I was from?*
>
> *Where I'm from, Puerto Rico stays on our minds*
> *when the fresh breeze of café con leche y pan con*
> *mantequilla comes through our half-open windows*
> *and under our doors while the sun starts to rise.*

Prompt: Consider the scents, sounds, and textures of a place you or your character is from. Begin your writing with the phrase, "I am from…" What does it mean to be from a scent, a memory, a color, a sound, a texture?

Conversations with the Body

HOW ALIVE ARE YOU WILLING TO BET

We who are survivors of trauma have learned to both pay close attention to and completely ignore our bodies—and we can use writing as a way to reengage in a sometimes long-overdue conversation with our physical selves.

Our bodies hold a great deal of our experience: some we can find words for, some that live still unspoken within us, and some that will forever be without language.

Think about a time before now when you experienced a big emotion—joy, grief, fear, rage, lust, or another.

Take a moment to scan through your body, in your mind, as you think about that time. Is there a part of your body that seems to "come alive" when you think about that feeling?

Where did this emotion live in your body? How did you release it physically or hold it in? Did you allow yourself to express this emotion to others?

Give yourself about fifteen minutes to write about the feelings your body carries: how did it feel to carry that emotion then? What if you could express it now?

(Sometimes working with the first-person "I" in a prompt like this one feels too daunting or just doesn't click. In that case, think about changing the pronoun from *my* to *her/their/his*, the plural *our*, or the second-person *your*. Notice whether the writing flows more smoothly with this change.)

The poem "Fairy Tale" by Sheila Nickerson begins like this:

> *You wake one morning*
> *with a swan's wing for an arm.*

For this prompt, create two lists: along the right side of a page, make a list of ten parts of the human body; along the left side of the same page, write a list of ten parts of animals' bodies.

As randomly as you can, connect the items from each list with lines crisscrossing the page. Then, look at the pairs the lines have made: *hand—elephant trunk* or *thigh—bird wing*.

After you read through your pairs for a moment, let one of them choose you, and write for a few minutes about a situation where that part of the human body is replaced with that part of the animal body.

Then, set your timer for around fifteen minutes, and follow your writing wherever it seems to want you to go.

Myths and Truths

There are many misconceptions about trauma survivors, and those ideas can shape our understanding of ourselves, consciously or unconsciously.

When I say we can use a journaling practice to re-story ourselves, I mean we can discover what stories we tell routinely, what stories we have shaped ourselves around, and we can decide whether those stories still serve us. We can write new stories for ourselves and our lives.

Take a few moments and just write, one after another, some of the messages you've received about survivors of whatever trauma you experienced (or survivors in general), such as "She asked for it by the way she was dressed" or "He shouldn't have been in that neighborhood at night" or "If only you didn't make him mad."

Notice what comes up for you as you're writing down these cultural messages/myths. If you want to write back to one of the ideas, choose one and counter it, and, if you are drawn in another direction, follow the pull of your writing.

_____

_____

_____

_____

_____

_____

_____

_____

_____

_____

_____

_____

_____

_____

_____

_____

_____

_____

_____

_____

_____

_____

_____

_____

_____

_____

_____

_____

_____

One of the myths/truths about survivors is that we *lose our voices* in the course of the violence done to us. For a few of us, this is literally true. For many of us, however, we don't so much lose our voices as those around us lose the ability to hear us, to attend to our words, to pay attention, and take action on our behalf.

Consider your voice for a few minutes—what was the quality of your voice when you were a child? What about now? In what ways did you speak about what you were going through? How did your story emerge through your many languages (body, verbal, actions)?

Give yourself three minutes with each of these phrases:

> This is what my voice could do...
>
> This is what my voice could not do...
>
> This is what I wish my voice could have done...

Then, write for ten more minutes, and follow your writing wherever it seems to want you to go!

_____

_____

_____

_____

_____

_____

_____

_____

_____

_____

_____

_____

_____

_____

_____

_____

_____

_____

_____

_____

_____

_____

_____

_____

_____

_____

_____

Week Four

Reclaiming Voice

We're moving toward the midway point of our eight weeks together. How is this process feeling? How are you making room for your words every week? How are you being gentle with your fierce and tender self?

When I think about *fearless words*, I think about everything that's been written, that you have already written so far. Every single one of the words in this journal is fearless—because it takes great courage to put pen to paper, particularly when the words you write are easing into language memories, voices, or images we've rarely or never been able to speak about.

It's a bit of a misnomer, though: fearless words. I think most of us writing about violence or trauma done to us are afraid. Of course we are. We are afraid of being punished for saying these things—even when that saying is "only" on the page. These things were meant to be kept quiet. We are breaking their silences with this writing.

Someone said that being brave didn't mean being fearless—it meant feeling fear and acting anyway. Sometimes, that's exactly how we have to show up to the page: feeling the fear, the grief, the loss, and trusting our words anyway.

Considering all of this, begin writing from the phrase, "*If I told you what I was afraid to tell you…*"

(Is there a specific "you" you're imagining: sibling, lover, parent, therapist, doctor, roommate, other writers, self?)

(Remember: change *I* to *she* or *he* or *they* or *we* or *you* or…just find what clicks.)

_____

_____

_____

_____

_____

_____

_____

_____

_____

_____

_____

_____

_____

_____

_____

_____

_____

_____

_____

_____

_____

_____

_____

_____

_____

_____

_____

_____

_____

_____

_____

_____

_____

_____

_____

_____

_____

_____

_____

_____

_____

_____

_____

_____

_____

_____

_____

_____

Let's return to the myth we tackled during week three: the idea that survivors of sexual trauma lose their voices.

Although most of us retain the ability to speak, many of us know what it's like to have our words ignored or denied. As a result, we might find it difficult to say things we feel, speak up when we are hurt or angry, or tell truths we think others might have a difficult time hearing. We might feel like the words just won't come.

For this prompt, imagine reaching into your throat and physically pulling out blockages, then putting them down on the page. What do these blocks look like, smell like? What color or shape are they? What do they sound like?

What does it feel like to have them out of your throat?

What would you say, yell, whisper, or sing with those blocks gone?

Give yourself fifteen minutes. Follow your writing wherever it wants you to go.

_____

_____

_____

_____

_____

_____

_____

_____

_____

_____

_____

_____

_____

_____

_____

_____

_____

_____

_____

_____

_____

_____

_____

Writing into Spirit

Spirit, the idea of something outside ourselves that guides or assists or holds us, is complicated for many of us. Those of us raised in an organized religion might have negative associations with worship or God. Even more so for those of us abused within those traditions by spiritual "leaders."

Yet, many of us are still drawn to connect with an essence, idea, or being outside of and bigger than ourselves. Take a few moments to create a list of deities or representations of spirit— just let this be a brainstorm, and jot down ideas even if you have no intention of writing about them. (Examples that have shown up on lists include: God, Quan Yin, Jesus, Tree, Ocean, Song/ Music, Mary, Buddha, Muhammad, Ancestors, Eve…)

Let one of these words choose you, and imagine a conversation with that spirit, being, or concept. Perhaps the writer will address the spirit. Perhaps the spirit is the one speaking. Some writers will begin with the words, *"What I always wanted to tell you was…"* or *"What I always wanted you to tell me was…"*

_____

_____

_____

_____

_____

_____

_____

_____

_____

_____

_____

_____

_____

_____

_____

_____

_____

_____

_____

_____

_____

_____

_____

_____

What does "sacred space" mean to you?

A private corner of the house. A quiet spot in a meadow or under a tree. In the church right before or after services have concluded. In conversation with a beloved friend. At the oceanside. In the kitchen. At shabbat dinner. At prayer. At your writing table.

How often do you spend time in sacred space? Is your body sacred? Are there parts of you that feel sacred? If not, could you write about them as though they were?

Give yourself twelve to fifteen minutes, and write yourself into sacred space.

_____

_____

_____

_____

_____

_____

_____

_____

_____

_____

_____

_____

_____

_____

_____

_____

_____

_____

_____

_____

_____

_____

_____

_____

_____

_____

Week Six

Welcoming
Our Desire

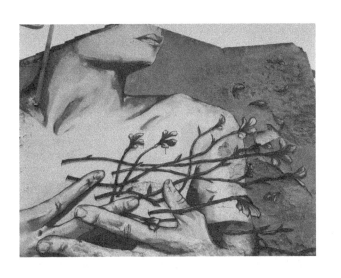

We who live in the aftermath of sexual violence have learned devastating "lessons" about sexuality: the way it can be used against us and wielded as a weapon. We may be shamed for our desire or made to believe the sexual violence was our fault. For a time, it may be safer to withdraw from sex. This is completely understandable.

But a healthy and joyful sexuality is our birthright if we choose it. Those who harmed us do not get to take that away from us.

One way to reconnect with our desire is to write about it—to first put onto the page words we are too nervous to speak aloud, to allow our characters to show us what playful, risky, and/or joyful sex looks like. In writing a character's body or longing, we experience it in our own bodies, slowly and gently reembodying what consensual, enjoyable sex can feel like.

Write a letter to a younger you about how you feel about your desire/sex at this point in your life: What's different for you now? What has surprised you? What do you still want?

You might also write a letter to yourself now, from a future self who has a more healed relationship with their desire: How did they get to where they are now? What do they hope for you?

One of the powerful pleasures of sex is getting to ask for what we want. Perhaps we have heard lectures at school or read "safer sex" guidance that tells us to be clear with our partners— we should only say yes when we mean yes and say no when we mean no.

But how do we, who have had to focus our attention only on the sexual desires of others, even *know* what we want?

Writing about our desires can be a way to explore them outside the charged context of a date or sexual encounter. We try something on, we watch a character doing what we imagined, and we notice what it feels like.

Consider writing a character who is discovering their own body: what kind of touch they like, what kind of touch doesn't work for them, what they ache or hunger for, what they never want again. How would they describe these learnings to a new partner or to someone who loved them for a long time?

You might begin with the phrase "These are the secrets of my body…"

If you feel stuck with this one, try writing in the third person— *the secrets of her body, their body, his body*—or in the plural—*the secrets of our body*.

Allow the writing to get as explicit as you're comfortable with, and follow your writing wherever it pulls you.

_____

_____

_____

_____

_____

_____

_____

_____

_____

_____

_____

_____

_____

_____

_____

_____

_____

_____

_____

_____

_____

_____

_____

_____

Reaching Back Through the Fire

Though many of us often feel alone, we have (or have had) guidance and support in many different forms, from counselors or therapists to book characters to artists and activists to online communities.

Think for a few minutes about those who gave you permission to survive.

Maybe someone spoke to you directly and said those words. Maybe you read a book or watched a movie about a character who went through something similar to you and you learned from them. Maybe it was a song, or a friend, or an animal.

Write about that person or those people, that character or work of art. Who or what inspires you to survive?

_____

_____

_____

_____

_____

_____

_____

_____

_____

_____

_____

_____

_____

_____

_____

_____

_____

_____

_____

_____

_____

_____

_____

_____

_____

_____

_____

_____

_____

_____

_____

_____

_____

_____

_____

_____

There is a poem I have shared often with writing groups, "For my young friends who are afraid" by William Stafford, which closes this way:

> *What you fear*
> *will not go away: it will take you into*
> *yourself and bless you and keep you.*
> *That's the world, and we all live there.*

I invite you to write a letter to a new survivor. What do you want to share with them? What do you wish you had known when you were beginning your journey? What helped you, and what do you want to offer forward to them?

(A "new survivor" can be someone of any age. I'm thinking about someone new to their recovery work, whether they were harmed recently or a long, long time ago.)

✎ _____

_____

_____

_____

_____

_____

_____

Radical Self-Care

So very many of us are not only not taught how to take care of ourselves, we are also taught not to take care of ourselves—we are trained to believe that self-care is selfish and indulgent and that we should always turn our attention to others' needs.

You may already be familiar with Black lesbian feminist Audre Lorde's words about self-care: "Caring for myself is not self-indulgence, it is self-preservation, and that is an act of political warfare."

Take a piece of paper and tear it into eight pieces. On each piece of paper, write one of the following words: *self-love*, *rest*, *open*, *leap*, *love*, *peace*, *ease*, *risk*. Then, fold up the papers, hold them in your hands, close your eyes for the span of a deep breath, and then choose one of those pieces of paper. Unfold it, and insert the word you've chosen into the following phrase: "*What if I deserved _____*"

Let that be the place where your writing begins. What does it mean to attend to, care for, or even adore what we (may) have been told was not worth loving?

_____

_____

_____

_____

_____

Have you been told you are too much, or not enough?

Consider these final lines from David Whyte's poem "Sweet Darkness"

> *Sometimes it takes darkness and the sweet*
> *confinement of your aloneness*
> *to learn*
>
> *anything or anyone*
> *that does not bring you alive*
>
> *is too small for you.*

If you'd like, first find and read the whole poem. When you're ready, take ten or fifteen minutes to write about what or who in your life is asking you to be smaller than you really are. What if you gently, with kindness and generosity, let those things or relationships go or shift into a different place? What would your life feel like then? What would it mean if you were enough, just as you are?

_____

_____

_____

_____

_____

_____

_____

_____

_____

_____

_____

_____

_____

_____

_____

_____

_____

_____

_____

_____

_____

_____

_____

_____

_____

_____

_____

_____

_____

Additional Prompts

We have finished our eight weeks of guided writing together, but that doesn't mean your practice, your writing, is finished.

Here are some additional prompts—further sparks for your writer's imagination (you can find many prompts in *Writing Ourselves Whole* as well):

- Maybe you want to begin a new process with this topic: What aren't we supposed to write about? Create a list of taboo topics. Then, choose one to write about. Begin with the phrase: "I'm not supposed to tell you…" or "I'm not supposed to write about…"

- Take five to seven minutes with each of the following themes: "What they told me to say" and "What they told me not to say."

- Write about the stories you tell. Then, write about the stories you don't tell.

- "What is a survivor?" Write the question, then answer it, then write the question again, then answer again— repeat this process for four minutes, then set a timer for ten minutes and write whatever comes to mind. (This is a variation of the "begin again" prompt in *Writing Ourselves Whole*.)

- What love song would your body sing to you?

- Write for five minutes about each of these: your hands as an infant; your hands as a seven-year-old; your hands as a seventeen-year-old; your hands at your age now.

- What are you not grateful for? What are you grateful for?

- Journal about the following quotations:

  - "Our lives begin to end the day we become silent about things that matter," (Dr. Martin Luther King, Jr.).

  - "And when you have found your voice, you must take it to the center of the city," (*The Odyssey*).

- Write about where you have not belonged. Then write about where you do, or could, belong.

Keep going, keep healing, keep discovering, keep playing, keep writing, keep writing, keep writing:

_____

_____

_____

_____

_____

_____

_____

_____

_____

_____

Further Reading About Writing and Transformation

It starts with your heart
and radiates out

Anzaldúa, Gloria. *Borderlands/La Frontera: The New Mestiza*. Spinsters/Aunt Lute, 1987.

Bass, Ellen and Laura Davis. *The Courage to Heal: A Guide for Women Survivors of Child Sexual Abuse*. Third Edition. Harper Perennial, 1994.

Cameron, Julia. *The Artist's Way: A Spiritual Path to Higher Creativity*. Tarcher, 1992.

Cross, Jen. *Writing Ourselves Whole: Using the Power of Your Own Creativity to Recover and Heal from Sexual Trauma*. Mango, 2017.

Goldberg, Natalie. *Writing Down the Bones: Freeing the Writer Within*. Shambhala, 1986.

Hanes, Staci. *The Survivor's Guide to Sex: How to Have an Empowered Sex Life after Child Sexual Abuse*. Cleis Press, 1999.

Herman, Judith. *Trauma and Recovery: The Aftermath of Violence—from Domestic Violence to Political Abuse*. Basic Books, 1997.

Lamott, Anne. *Bird by Bird: Some Instructions on Writing and Life*. Anchor Books, 1995.

Lorde, Audre. *Sister Outsider*. The Crossing Press, 1984.

Pennebaker, James. *Opening Up: The Healing Power of Confiding in Others*. William Morrow and Co., 1990.

Schneider, Pat. *Writing Alone and with Others*. Oxford University Press, 2003.

van Dernoot Lipsky, Laura and Connie Burke. *Trauma Stewardship: An Everyday Guide to Caring for Self While Caring for Others*. Berrett-Koehler Publishers, 2009.

About Jen

For over fifteen years, Jen Cross has facilitated writing workshops focused on sexuality and for sexual trauma survivors. Jen is a strong believer in writing's power to transform and release the as-yet-unlanguaged experiences we hold inside. Jen is the author of *Writing Ourselves Whole: Using the Power of Your Own Creativity to Recover and Heal from Sexual Trauma* (Mango, 2017), and the novella *Night Hands* (The Massachusetts Review Working Titles Series, 2019). She's the co-editor of *Sex Still Spoken Here: An Erotic Reading Circle Anthology*

(CSC Press, 2014), the editor of two Writing Ourselves Whole anthologies (*Fierce Hunger* and *Wicked Words*), and the author of four chapbooks (*notorious*, *what they didn't teach us*, *pink & dangerous*, and *unconsummated*). Jen's writing appears in over fifty anthologies and periodicals, including *Nobody Passes*, *The Healing Art of Writing 2010*, *Under the Gum Tree*, *The Elephants*, *Sinister Wisdom*, *Visible: A Femmethology (Vol. 1)*, and *Best Sex Writing 2008*.

In 2003, Jen founded Writing Ourselves Whole, and she has worked with hundreds of writers through private workshops and in collaboration with colleges, social change organizations, and other institutions throughout the US, including at Stanford University, Wesleyan University, the University of California at Davis, Dartmouth College, the University of California at San Francisco, Brown University, Goddard College, the University of Oregon at Eugene, Evergreen State University. She has also partnered with the Femme Conference, Survivorship and the Survivorship annual conference, San Francisco Women Against Rape, Bay Area Women Against Rape, and Community United Against Violence.

Jen holds an MFA in Creative Writing from San Francisco State University and an MA in Transformative Language Arts from Goddard College and has been awarded residencies at Hedgebrook and the Kimmel Harding Nelson Art Center.

For more information, visit writingourselveswhole.org and jencross.net.

Mango Publishing, established in 2014, publishes an eclectic list of books by diverse authors—both new and established voices—on topics ranging from business, personal growth, women's empowerment, LGBTQ studies, health, and spirituality to history, popular culture, time management, decluttering, lifestyle, mental wellness, aging, and sustainable living. We were recently named 2019's #1 fastest growing independent publisher by Publishers Weekly. Our success is driven by our main goal, which is to publish high quality books that will entertain readers as well as make a positive difference in their lives.

Our readers are our most important resource; we value your input, suggestions, and ideas. We'd love to hear from you—after all, we are publishing books for you!

Please stay in touch with us and follow us at:

Facebook: Mango Publishing
Twitter: @MangoPublishing
Instagram: @MangoPublishing
LinkedIn: Mango Publishing
Pinterest: Mango Publishing

Sign up for our newsletter at www.mangopublishinggroup.com and receive a free book!

Join us on Mango's journey to reinvent publishing, one book at a time.